DEPARTMENT OF JUSTICE
FELINE BUREAU OF INVESTIGATION
FIDELITY BRAVERY CATNIP

FBI'S MOST WANTED CATS

MARK LEIGH

summersdale

Summersdale Publishers Ltd
46 West Street
Chichester
West Sussex
PO19 1RP
UK

www.summersdale.com

Printed and bound in China

ISBN: 978-1-84953-294-5

Substantial discounts on bulk quantities of Summersdale books are available to corporations, professional associations and other organisations. For details telephone Summersdale Publishers on (+44-1243-771107), fax (+44-1243-786300) or email (nicky@summersdale.com).

1' 6"

1' 0"

FBI'S MOST WANTED CATS

From an original idea by
Mark Leigh & Mike Lepine

MARK LEIGH

ABOUT THE AUTHOR

The author and
Maxwell Woofington III

Surrey-based author Mark Leigh has written or co-written over forty humour and trivia books on subjects as diverse as millionaires, extraterrestrials, the Conservative Party and toilets (none of which are connected… although it sounds like they could be).

He has worked with the great and the good, including Julian Clary, Rolf Harris, Ade Edmondson, Des Lynam, Chris Tarrant and even Roy 'Chubby' Brown. TV projects have included scriptwriting for Joe Pasquale, Jeremy Beadle, Noel Edmonds, Hale & Pace, Brian Conley, Jimmy Tarbuck and Bobby Davro. His comedy novel *Dick Longg Saves the World!* is available on Kindle, while his works in progress include two film scripts.

Mark is an authority on badly behaved pets, being the owner of the naughtiest dog in the world, Maxwell Woofington III.

www.mark-leigh.com

INTRODUCTION

Feline Felons, Pussy Perpetrators or Kitty Criminals…

Whatever you call them, this motley collection of moggies has one thing in common: they're all on the FBI's* Most Wanted list.

Sure, they may look cute, cuddly and even comical but appearances are deceptive. These cats have been responsible for some of the most heinous and shocking crimes ever committed, from breaking and entering a goldfish bowl and possession of catnip with intent to supply to unravelling a ball of wool with malicious intent. What's more, despite the best efforts of law enforcement officials and numerous 'Wanted' and 'Lost' posters pinned to trees, all these cats are still at large. They could be hiding out anywhere: in your garage, curled up at the bottom of a laundry basket or even snuggled in a ball under your bed…

So if you spot Chairman Meow, Sidney Snuggles, Poopkins or any of these other feline fugitives, you are advised not to approach them. Be warned; these cats are clawed and dangerous!

*Feline Bureau of Investigation

FELINE BUREAU OF INVESTIGATION

Name:
Marc Anthony

Aliases:
Fat Tony

Crime:
Illegal loitering on next door's lawn with intent to poop

Notes:
Considered large and extremely heavy. Thought to be the 'Mr Big' of kitty lawn fouling.

FELINE BUREAU OF INVESTIGATION

Name:
Dave

Aliases:
The Professor

Crime:
Obtaining treats by deception

Notes:
Wrote the book on extorting cat snacks.
Master of the hypnotic stare; do not look
into his eyes.

FELINE BUREAU OF INVESTIGATION

Name:
Gingie

Aliases:
Don Catleone

Crime:
Possession of catnip with intent to supply

Notes:
Runs the East Side Catnip Cartel. Any feline that crosses him ends up with a mouse's head in their basket.

FELINE BUREAU OF INVESTIGATION

Name:
Poopkins

Aliases:
Mr P

Crime:
Unravelling a ball of wool with malicious intent

Notes:
Responsible for the destruction of at least five sweaters.
Also wanted for questioning about the mutilation of a cable-knit cardigan.

FELINE BUREAU OF INVESTIGATION

Name:
Anastasia

Aliases:
The Magpie, Raffles

Crime:
Jewel theft

Notes:
One of the most audacious cat burglars ever.

The brains behind the Great Diamond Tiara Heist from 11 Oakington Road.

FELINE BUREAU OF INVESTIGATION

Name:
Gingernut

Aliases:
The Nutster

Crime:
First-degree laziness

Notes:
Has been known to impersonate a sloth.
Personal mantra is 'Just because I need to,
doesn't mean I have to.'

FELINE BUREAU OF INVESTIGATION

Name:
Stewie

Aliases:
The Guvnor

Crime:
Grand theft sausage

Notes:
Specialises in meat-based robberies.
Also wanted for lamb larceny.

FELINE BUREAU OF INVESTIGATION

Name:
Boomerang

Aliases:
Chief

Crime:
Forced entry and trespass

Notes:
Enters premises searching for snacks using a combination of his natural cat agility and his unnatural knowledge of lock-picking.

FELINE BUREAU OF INVESTIGATION

Name:
Romeow

Aliases:
Luvva Boi

Crime:
Lewd conduct

Notes:
Displays butt hole in the presence of minors.
Has been also known to lick his crotch area in a manner likely to deprave and corrupt.

FELINE BUREAU OF INVESTIGATION

Name:
Ric Roc

Aliases:
The Cat That Got The Cream, Moggie The Milk

Crime:
Unlawful tampering with a milk carton

Notes:
Also wanted in connection with an unsuccessful raid on a crème fraîche factory.

Used to run with the Lactic Bandits.
Believed to have switched allegiance to their rivals, the Pasteurised Pussies.

FELINE BUREAU OF INVESTIGATION

Name:
Tiddles

Aliases:
T-Bone, Mr T

Crime:
Climbing a Christmas tree without the owner's consent

Notes:
Responsible for bauble breakage and fairy light entanglement.
Seasonal criminal; active between 15 December and 6 January.

FELINE BUREAU OF INVESTIGATION

Name:

Chairman Meow

Aliases:

Tux, Catkins, Smarty-Pants

Crime:

Furball felony

Notes:

Also wanted for aggravated regurgitation. Subject to a restraining order preventing him from retching within 3 metres of his owners, or when they are eating.

FELINE BUREAU OF INVESTIGATION

Name:
Adolf

Aliases:
Kitler, The Feline Führer

Crime:
Hate crime

Notes:
Victimisation of ginger cats.
His political ideology can be found in
his book, *Mein Kat*.

FELINE BUREAU OF INVESTIGATION

Name:
Tabitha

Aliases:
Scratcher

Crime:
Criminal damage aided and abetted by very sharp claws

Notes:
Should be considered clawed and extremely scratchy.
Has been in and out of Kitten Offenders' Institutions since she was two months old.

FELINE BUREAU OF INVESTIGATION

Name:
Falafel

Aliases:
The Chlorophyll Gobbler

Crime:
Plant-eating misdemeanours

Notes:
Suspected of tree bark stripping in three counties.
Last seen in the vicinity of the Chelsea Flower Show.

FELINE BUREAU OF INVESTIGATION

Name:
Moggles

Aliases:
Sir Purralot

Crime:
Being too cute

Notes:
Also wanted on twelve counts of being excessively endearing.
Actions include leaping at butterflies, chasing leaves, pawing at his reflection and sitting in a shoe.

FELINE BUREAU OF INVESTIGATION

Name:
King Ralph

Aliases:
Maj

Crime:
Malicious jealousy of new babies

Notes:
Distinctive green eyes.
Considered the jealous type and extremely smothery.
Is only allowed supervised access to newborns.

FELINE BUREAU OF INVESTIGATION

Name:
 Sidney Snuggles

Aliases:
 Sid Vicious

Crime:
 Hissing with intent to intimidate

Notes:
 Suffers from anger management issues.
 Has three priors for threatening
 behaviour and spitting in an enclosed
 space.

FELINE BUREAU OF INVESTIGATION

Name:
Nugget

Aliases:
Nug-Nug

Crime:
Excessive playfulness early on a
Sunday morning

Notes:
Wakes owners at 6 a.m. to obtain
playtime under duress.
Blames his actions on the condition
EMF (Early Morning Friskiness).

FELINE BUREAU OF INVESTIGATION

Name:
Oddball

Aliases:
Oddie, Ugmo, The Gimp

Crime:
Looking weird

Notes:
Considered the prime suspect in a recent spate of anti-wrinkle cream thefts. Has a reputation for upsetting small children.

FELINE BUREAU OF INVESTIGATION

Name:
Mr Furry

Aliases:
Tigger

Crime:
Conspiracy to jump on table or other work surface without warning

Notes:
Currently wanted for ruining a family dinner and knocking tea over a keyboard. Received a suspended sentence for disrupting homework.

FELINE BUREAU OF INVESTIGATION

Name:
Munchkin

Aliases:
Heidi

Crime:
Unlawfully absconding from home

Notes:
Has been known to lie low in sheds, garages and outside playhouses.
Has been on the run for fourteen days, despite twenty 'Missing' posters pinned to trees.

FELINE BUREAU OF INVESTIGATION

Name:
Bonetti

Aliases:
The Cat

Crime:
Causing aggravated distress to owners

Notes:
Deviously conceals himself in hidey-holes around the house before leaping out without warning.
Has been known to stowaway to avoid extradition.

FELINE BUREAU OF INVESTIGATION

Name:
Bert and Ernie

Aliases:
The Brothers

Crime:
Fencing stolen cat treats

Notes:
Stolen treats are passed both over and through fences.
Their criminal motto is: 'If you've got a snack, we've got a buyer.'

FELINE BUREAU OF INVESTIGATION

Name:
Sasparilla

Aliases:
Sassy

Crime:
Obstructing a laptop with intent to annoy

Notes:
Crimes include document deletion with menace. Also known as 'Kitten on the Keys'.

FELINE BUREAU OF INVESTIGATION

Name:
Bobo

Aliases:
Paws

Crime:
Beef burglary

Notes:
Believed to head up the band of kitty
thieves, The Sirloin Purloiners.
The prime suspect in the theft of prime cuts.

FELINE BUREAU OF INVESTIGATION

Name:
Muffin

Aliases:
Top Cat

Crime:
Trafficking class A cat snacks

Notes:
Leader of the East Side Kitties.
Is always accompanied by two
bodyguards.

FELINE BUREAU OF INVESTIGATION

Name:
Sailor Sam

Aliases:
Matey

Crime:
Crimes against fashion

Notes:
Wanted for bringing the reputation of
elegant felines into disrepute.
Favourite designer brands are Hissey
Miyake, Catkin Klein and Purrberry.

FELINE BUREAU OF INVESTIGATION

Name:
  Joe

Aliases:
  Joe Schmo

Crime:
  Loitering in doorways with intent to trip

Notes:
  Also wanted for obstruction; habitually lies down in places likely to cause an accident.
  Responsible for causing at least four broken wrists, two fractured arms and a bruised ego.

FELINE BUREAU OF INVESTIGATION

Name:

Michelangelo

Aliases:

'Mad' Mike, Rambo Cat

Crime:

Illegal operation of a private army

Notes:

Believed to lead a crack squad of
Moggie Mercenaries.
Veteran of numerous catfights.

FELINE BUREAU OF INVESTIGATION

Name:
Fluffy

Aliases:
Furrocious

Crime:
Second-degree moulting

Notes:
Sheds fur with complete disregard for carpets, rugs and clothing.
Also wanted for hairball misdemeanours.

FELINE BUREAU OF INVESTIGATION

Name:
Miss Everpurr

Aliases:
Itchy

Crime:
Providing a safe haven for fleas and mites

Notes:
Also wanted for illegally harbouring ticks.
Previous conviction for possessing ringworm.

FELINE BUREAU OF INVESTIGATION

Name:
  Sheba

Aliases:
  Queenie

Crime:
  Staring at owner in the bath in a
  manner likely to cause distress and
  embarrassment

Notes:
  Demonstrates complete lack of fear of
  water.
  Also known for making owner feel
  extremely self-conscious on the toilet.

FELINE BUREAU OF INVESTIGATION

Name:
Merlin

Aliases:
Hocus Pocus

Crime:
Unlawful concealment

Notes:
Fearless. Will put his life in jeopardy in the pursuit of a new hiding place.
His MO includes hiding in wheelie bins, under floorboards and in the fireplace.

FELINE BUREAU OF INVESTIGATION

Name:
Smokey

Aliases:
Dozy, Zee Zee

Crime:
Fraudulent catnapping

Notes:
Infamous kitty con artist.
Fakes sleep in order to remain on comfiest sofa or bed.

FELINE BUREAU OF INVESTIGATION

Name:
Precious

Aliases:
Miss P

Crime:
Obstructing a public highway

Notes:
Exhibits wilful contempt for other road users.
Also wanted for peeing on a traffic policeman's boot.

FELINE BUREAU OF INVESTIGATION

Name:
Titch

Aliases:
Stinker

Crime:
Drinking water from a toilet bowl without consent

Notes:
Has also been known to lick the Cif toilet block.

Homeowners within a 2-mile radius are advised to keep the seat down at all times.

FELINE BUREAU OF INVESTIGATION

Name:
  Scout

Aliases:
  Spidercat

Crime:
  Wasting emergency services' time

Notes:
  Infamous for incessant tree climbing.
  Has also managed to get stuck at the
  top of five telegraph poles, three mobile
  phone masts and a municipal fountain.

FELINE BUREAU OF INVESTIGATION

Name:
Tyler

Aliases:
Boom Boom

Crime:
Illegal cage fighting

Notes:
The brains behind the Feline Fight Club.
Expert in MMMA (Moggie Mixed
Martial Arts); black belt in Kitty Karate
and Cat Fu.

FELINE BUREAU OF INVESTIGATION

Name:
Jessie

Aliases:
Catastrophe

Crime:
Reckless scratching likely to endanger sofa

Notes:
Linked to numerous cases of armchair mauling.

Subject of a restraining order taken out by a chain of furniture shops.

FELINE BUREAU OF INVESTIGATION

Name:
  Gee Willikers

Aliases:
  Snatch

Crime:
  Abduction and false imprisonment

Notes:
  Chief suspect in the catnapping of Big Ted.
  Ransom demands included fifteen tins
  of chicken and tuna chunks and a new
  scratching post.

FELINE BUREAU OF INVESTIGATION

Name:

Gizmo

Aliases:

Jimmy The Weasel

Crime:

Peeping Tom

Notes:

Also wanted for indecent exposure.
Currently on the Kitten Offenders'
Register.

FELINE BUREAU OF INVESTIGATION

Name:
  Lucky

Aliases:
  Pouncer

Crime:
  Unlawful littering

Notes:
  Leaves mouse remains all around
  house.
  Has used sweet demeanour to get away
  with murder. Literally.

THANK YOU

Mark would like to thank the following people for their suggestions, assistance and/or tea and chocolate Hobnobs:

Darin Jewel

Barney Leigh

Debbie Leigh

Polly Leigh

Mike Lepine

Anna Martin

PHOTO CREDITS

Marc Anthony - HelleM
Dave - Melanie DeFazio
Gingie - Aptyp_koK
Poopkins - Ariusz Nawrocki
Anastasia - Artem Kursin
Gingernut - Vera Kailova
Stewie - Gladkova Svetlana
Boomerang - Aliaksei Lasevich
Romeow - GJS
Ric Roc - Peter Radacsi
Tiddles - slon1971
Chairman Meow - MAErtek
Adolf - Jordan Tan
Tabitha - 9744444159
Falafel - Olga Miltsova
Moggles - Linn Currie
King Ralph - gengirl
Sidney Snuggles - Elena Borisova
Nugget - Tom Pingel
Oddball - Rudchenko Liliia
Mr Furry - Dirk Ott

If you're interested in finding out more about our humour books follow us on Twitter:
@SummersdaleLOL

www.summersdale.com